To Gail & Lee
Enjoy these words
from the heart.

# PERENNIAL SECRETS

## Poetry & Prose

By

## JENNIFER SMITH TURNER

*Jennifer Smith Turner*

ISBN: 1-4107-4334-9 (Paperback)
ISBN: 1-4107-4335-7 (Dust Jacket)

Library of Congress Control Number: 2003093245


This book is printed on acid free paper.


Printed in the United States of America


Cover photograph by the author
Author photo by Eric V. Turner


www.jennifersmithturner.com


Second Printing 1/2004

*For my mother,*
*Margaree L. Smith,*
*a truly phenomenal woman.*

*1928-2000*

## PSALM 23
*A psalm of David*

*The Lord is my shepherd, I shall not want.*
*He makes me lie down in green pastures,*
*he leads me beside quiet waters,*
*he restores my soul,*
*He guides me in paths of righteousness*
*for his name sake.*
*Even though I walk*
*through the valley of the shadow of death,*
*I will fear no evil,*
*for you are with me;*
*your rod and your staff,*
*they comfort me.*

*You prepare a table before me*
*in the presence of my enemies.*
*You anoint my head with oil;*
*my cup overflows.*
*Surely goodness and love will follow me*
*all the days of my life,*
*and I will dwell in the house of the Lord*
*forever.*

# Acknowledgements

My thanks to the editor of the *Martha's Vineyard Gazette* for publishing the following poems: *Tree* and *Nine Eleven.*

I also thank Westmeadow Press for including the poem, *Color of Language,* in **Vineyard Poets**, an anthology of poems by Vineyard writers.

A very special "thank you" to family and friends: faithful readers and listeners whose comments, love and support, have helped me pave a poetic path sprinkled with secrets.

# Perennial Secrets

*If you tell a secret, is it secret no more?*

# CONTENTS

Perennial Secrets

Jennifer Smith Turner

Martha's Vineyard Garden

# Black is Beautiful

# Color of Language

He thought it was safe
To finally say, *Ain't*.
Proud man
Crayola skin
Licorice stick colors
Most leave in box for another.

Little did he know
World said *no*.
Slang…you…will not go.
O.K. for majority lawyer,
sportscaster, entertainer;
symbol - engaged in the world.
Not you brown eyed child
For you accusation
*less than…outside…foreign…street.*

He thought it was safe
To finally say, *Ain't*.
Without skipping beat.

Little did he know
World *still* said no.
Ain't gonna dis us so,
We - who taught you to speak.

*Dis…what?*
Now he *knew* it was safe
To finally say, *Ain't*.
But I no longer want to
Been stolen from me
Not going to speak like thee.

Little did he know
World would say, *Ho!*
Say it ain't so
Licorice stick thinks he better than we?

He thought it *must* finally
be safe to say, *Ain't.*

*Assuming he was free...*

Little did he know?
World said, *Hell no!*
It ain't so.
Will not be.

He sighed—
Perhaps for the children
If not me.

# Home

What do you call a row house without rows?

Neighborhood ghosts call children's games—
Hide n' seek, hop scotch, marbles, tag
Giggles, cries of summers' long sultry days
Sidewalks teem - little people born in post-war bubble
anticipate free world without trouble.

Plastic sealed furniture echo family lives
Photographed walls record images—blood ties.
Souls march through time
Generation after generation in line
Faces smile, plan history to come
Eyes frozen too early—future undone.

Thick smoke clouds proclaim civil rights
Brick by brick neighborhood no more
Stone by stone children no more
Bullet by bullet innocent no more
Town fathers' brief sabbatical from corruption;
Sagging, boarded rows come down!
Sunshine touches earth where darkness lives.
Parasites move, crawl on, seek new vistas to give.

What do *you* call a row house without rows?

Sentinel of life
Standing majestic
Guarding history

Aunt, God-Mother, friend shines alone—

*"You call it home baby, it is my home."*

# Black is Beautiful

Deep, dark as night
Glimmering like a lone star
Pale as the sun at dusk
Enchanting as a moonlit lake

# Accept This

Realities played upon by the mind
Cause distortion
Absurdity.
Accept what you see
You will not see anything else.
Delving deeper leads you to lose sight of it.

# Children

They come like whirls of dry sand
Attack your face, eyes.
In the midst of these stinging confrontations
You are blind to them.
They engulf you
Yet their twirling beings - translucent to you.

You doubt them.
Their minds travel a path alien to you.
You accuse, distrust—unwittingly.
Only when gusts of sand have passed;
Are you able to see them?

Then the children
Are not with you.

# Youth

Running rampart, running wild
A restless sea, savage beast

Running free oft' beguiled
A fleeting eagle, lonely child

Running far, running scared
On a bet, on a dare

Run alone, run with me
Run, run, run to be

# Invitation

# First Love

There amidst the flowers it steals,
passes slowly discreetly.
Takes from them—sweetness, newness.
It has also given these
Yet in giving, taking is molded, intertwined.
Living and dying are as one.

Meadows speak of its comings, goings
Orchestrating a symphony
Excitement springs into being.
Brilliance of such harmony beckons,
draws instruments to crescendo.

Perfumed breezes run free
Fill life giving life; touches them,
Moves the delicateness of their being
in anticipation of the end.

# Wind Asked Me

Wind asked me—
Go with him, fly, sail free.
He asked me - trust him
become one.

I told him no
I was not able to
I am not free.
The burden I carry
weighs me down to the ground.
I cannot be one with him
I am different than he.

He left me—
Beckoned a fair-haired lady
come fly with him.
She dropped her basket of roses
Shed her silken dress
And did fly.

# Not To Be Forgotten

There are many memories
collected over a lifetime.
Moments resurface from familiar scent, scene.
We are keepers of things
stored upon our mind's eye.

We clutter the attic of our memories.
Always searching for what has been lost
The collection is never ending,
ever present, always fading.

But for all time, all past moments;
for me there is but one lingering thought of you
One impression will shadow all else.

There is night terror.
Whistling wind, creaking floor board,
scent of liquor
Returns me
Hurtling back to what should never have been.

The attic must be cleaned.
Discard things of little value.
Dust, organize make room for new things.

The least valuable is somehow most important
Most difficult to let go.
Tucked away.
Filed among *not to be forgotten* memorabilia.

Just in case...

# Blind Solitude

I do not like this Blackness.
It seeps into the caverns of my mind,
traps me.

My eyes strain for a thread of light
This darkness envelops as a blanket.

I can touch this Blackness.
I reach out,
Feel cool cold emptiness.
I see velvet rich blackness
It eludes me.

My fingers seem to touch the fourth dimension.
I lose sight of them in my quest
to capture this blackness. .

Everything comes alive
But I cannot see!
My mind imagines gross
and grotesque creatures
This Blackness is a wall
upon which I continuously frantically
beat my head praying for light.

Black is beautiful!

But I do not like this blackness.
It is too deep.
Too solid.
Too immense.

It frightens me.
I fear...
This Blackness is forever.

# Hope

A burning desire to survive
A fine thin thread to cling
A sweet imaginary taste of good times
A determination to rise up in the apex of despair

# Leftovers

Peeking—underneath others,

Walking shorts not worn enough
no longer wearable;
blue cashmere sweater
better each decade, always in style,
snake like belt sporting new hole
half inch from it's tip.

Two lives begin to merge
Move familiar things to unfamiliar spaces
Convinced comfort will come in new places.

Yellow...faded...stuck together
Mirror life that was
Smiles promise full future
Eyes too young - unsure
Three pair frozen in time since then
Mothers, brother/son

What to do with these leftovers?

Hide
Throw away
Pretend

Remnants of life, part of me.
Let go...hold on
Store on history shelf - for me? No.
Who I am. Peeking...

# Invitation

When you have the time
Come to me
Let me share my love
Do not be fearful
Love is undemanding—
Most often

If you tear down walls
Let emotion free
You may find love for me—
When you have the time

# Navigation

If you truly love me...that thing you fear
haunts you while driving hearing
unsolicited navigation sounds—

*this turn - slow down babe - look out - easy*
*not this street the next - we...are...going...the...wrong...way*
*let's stop - ask for directions!*

That thing would not define your thoughts, tenderness
as we lay in bed; me wondering how a king-sized
can suddenly feel large as the ocean,
only faint glimpses of you at a distant shore.
You would merely tell me—

*For thirty years I navigated through light,*
*no fear, just shear delight, without you in my sight.*

Then hold me tight at night.
If you truly love me.

# Good Morning

Good morning?
Announce the close of sleep filled dreams
gentle resting from time now past.
*Good*—oh sets morning tone
good to have slept with you,
shared bed, pillow, touched, caressed,
good to open eyelids as one,
stretch evening from limbs, embrace new day
good to have you in my life
Good morning!

Then again *morning*, absent *good*—
jury verdict proclaimed!
Life sentence lays in wait.
Oh the small things…
Good morning, my love!

# Small Things

Of course small things shape
whole complex beings that touch earth, see stars.
You on bended knee hold my ankle.
Gently rub suntanned smooth skin;
cause body fluids to flow once again
move along intended path to sustain life.
Lips tenderly press against flesh,
unfamiliar crease, ankle meeting foot
that has walked many miles; many life miles;
many empty miles now suddenly full.
You comfort...
I wonder...
How many ankles in the universe
have known such bliss?
Two lips' gentle kiss.

# Ode to Bed

King be damned!
Promise more comfort, space
What a sham.

Comfort, elusive
Space, overrated
Better - close - sated.

Ah, Queen…
Welcome your highness!
In you, no escape
Middle of night,
Without sensuous bite

Limbs embrace
Arms entwine
Closeness - just fine.

# First Anniversary

Oh glorious day!
Laughter, joy
Warm soothing blanket of coziness surrounds me.
Hush of tranquil stillness envelopes my heart, mind.
Bursts of wonder, oh sweet happiness, tickle
Form crease lines on the corners of my lips.
Deep pools of gray green eyes dance, sparkle, proclaim—
*World - welcome, come join, partake!*

I have dreamt these things
Young child filled with hope, anticipation
Young woman in midst of pain, confusion, searching
I have longed for these feelings
In aftermath of loss, surrounded by emptiness.

I have prayed for this happiness
Standing in the epicenter of grief
Mourning child's memories.

Beneath the branches of a majestic cedar tree
Crows caw, gentle breeze kisses cheeks.
Unseeing eyes watch from above
Heart full of love, pride
One final wish has come true

*Be happy my daughter!*

Showers, magical rainbow
Dances across the heavens
Touches sea, lighthouse, bouquet of colors.
Revelers whisper of things to come.
Bubbles levitate, skip across air,
Kiss our face, hair

We are one…

# Anniversary Two

When did it become true?
At the moment of—I do
Or first at—I will
As early as—How are you

Perhaps while counting in twos
As naturally as arms, legs feet do
Sitting on the shore sapphire blue
Napping away hours, future moments in view

Maybe at 2 a.m.—tired too through
Unable to rollover, ignore, it is just you
On cold harsh tile
Wishing for stomach new
Twenty digits join forces
To get through night flu

Whatever you need, I will do

For certain it was true
Belly full with warm stew
Toes dance beneath blanket—colorful hue
Room filled with silence—soft morning dew

Moment most true—
With you…

# Be Free

# Awakening

Wake up, wake up!
Your fiftieth is here
In your twenties and thirties
It never seemed near
Wake up my dear
Your fiftieth is here

Celebrate!

Your life has grown this far
Many doors have been ajar
You peeked each one
Stepped in and out till done
Ever looking for the sun

Little boy in your wallet sleeve
Busy youngster playing on knees
Has found the sunshine door
How lucky for me!
Awake, the future is here!

# Graduate

Listen...
  Do you hear it?
Look...
  Can you see it?
Wait...
  It approaches
  Nexus youth and adulthood
  Beginnings, endings.

It surrounds us
Speaks of tireless days
Long nights.
Minds search
Souls connect
Design paths to future light.

Remember...
  Heartbeat first day
  Taps tune anxious anticipation

Recall...
  Welcomes, goodbyes
  Histories shared, plans divulged
  Feelings unspoken.

Imagine...
  Rainbow differences
  Masks of protection
  Hide real, wait for comfort.

Embrace...
  Memories created as one
  Life's architect vision
  Plan, design passages to come.

Let go, hold on, *begin!*

# Be Free

Beautiful mysterious package
Extravagant ribbons, bows
Shiny colorful paper...

All beckoning
Whispering
Of the gift inside.

Intoxicating this gift
This well dressed package of surprise...

Ignore it?
Walk away?
How to resist, why?

Wrappings—ribbons—bows
Like beauty of medusa
Costly splendor to fix your eyes upon
Touch, desire, enter.

*I own you...*
    *My way, my time...*
        *Freedom be gone...*
            *Choices few...*
                *Powerful force engulfs you...*

Beware!
Reach to have the gift
You lose to gain.
Leave ribbons—bows—clever wrapping
For someone else...

# Corporate-holic

I am a corporate-holic.
Work, work, work, work some more
Now, time to frolic.
Newspaper articles in view
Wall Street Journal, New York Times,
business sections I knew
"Most Powerful Black Execs"
My face, name nowhere to be seen
It should be, honestly I mean…

I am a corporate-holic.
Living life much more melodic.
Pinch me shake me lest I forget
politics, bureaucracy, tangled in nets.
Enron, WorldCom, Global Crossing
Anderson, Martha, others causing.
Hail kings, queens, chiefs
off with their heads, greedy cheats!

I am a corporate-holic.
Played game so well
knew how to call it
Learned from the best
Passed every test
Won prizes until…
time to rest.

I *was* a corporate-holic.
Walked away, saw it
Life - good
Pace - grand
Journey funded by plan
of corporate-holic.

I am poet…

# Hour Glass

It has a way of changing us
Takes away moments meant to remain
Our flesh is kissed by memory of these moments
Like sea touches sand

It is always there,
Moving, building, destroying
Creating creations that do not last,
Forming dreams which fade with the waking,
Building hopes that end unshaped.

Particles of sand speak of many days
Yet each imprint is brief
Minor disturbance cannot last
Untold, unnumbered ebbs and flows
Are kinder to the sand than this thing is to us.

# Act One

What became of her?
You ask
What became of her?
At last
She steals the show
In second act
Now the curtain comes down
Yes, act one curtain is down

# Butterflies

My body is a sieve
Pieces slowly
seep, creep, drip
into nothingness.
I am where I began
Small child - lighthearted - free.

My end - the beginning
My beginning - the end
Time between but a game
Time is timeless.

No longer unconscious being, patent mold
Formed without consent
Shaped without defense.

Time has come to form a new mold
The old tossed away
Carelessly - callously—happily—
forever changed!
Butterflies and me.

# Just Sit

# Bailey

*For DMA*

Heavy heart holds onto the scent of you
Aroma of childhood days
hanging in Mother's kitchen
Air laced with food of our history near and far.

Our seesaw of life once up then down
Always, you and I balance
move seamlessly through the decades
in harmony.

Now—the plank of wood
worn smooth through the years
is still, half empty, eyes missing.

Oh sweet brother, father, friend!
Connected in life…
So glad I had you at my side.
In my heart always.

My life journey
Continues…

# Memory

Somewhere in the recesses
Of my mind
Somewhere behind my eyelids
Late at night
Somewhere in my soul—
You are there
With me

# Just Sit

Just a blanket, piece of cloth really
Vibrant lapis lazuli
Hailing from Africa, India, Italy
Exotic place which gave birth to the cloth
for a traveler to bring home

Wrap around aging, ill shoulders
Warm an empty lap, impress visitors
Mask physical vulnerability during conversations
which skirt issues of life, death.

Just a cloth
Neatly folded,
hiding beneath the cushion of a chair.
Just a seat really.
That holds a prominent place.
Grandchildren, sons, daughters sit in the chair
Embrace essence of original womb
Ponder texture of storyteller tales
Drift into laughter
Whiff scent of favorite foods
Take pleasure in holiday gatherings
Float on tethered clouds of strength and courage.

Just cleaning one day.
Casually raise chair cushion
which has not been overturned
for too many years
Discover cloth - just a blanket really.

That keeps its place—
After popcorn kernels, lint, dust
have been sucked away—
Keeps its place beneath cushion of chair.
Just a seat, truly.

41

Where rolled tense as a kitten, first night
New pet for the family children
Who gently rub her fur
Let her know she is safe
Even though there no longer is suckling.

Where tight as a fur ball trembling—
I sit.

# Let Me Be

Come let me be infant kangaroo
Nestled in her pouch
Gentle bounces up down rock sweet memories
Into every inch of fur- sinew- cell
Preparation for changing bell.

Come let me be as waddling family members
March through space, little ones in tow
Unsteadily keeping pace
Nudged ever so gingerly
Rolling feathers dust shadow of what was.

Come let me be tender shell pierced
Chirping hunger at the sky
Beaks reach at nourishment so lovingly
Unconditionally brought alongside.

Come let me be mourner no more
Knowing it must never end
Yet sure there is place to spend—joy
In solitude, in time.

# The Stalker

Surprise…

It does not ask permission
Wait for the right moment
when you are prepared
No!
It dictates when - what time - where.

Ice water pours through you
Wrinkled skin of staying too long,
Weak arms hug empty chest
Swollen throat bellows silent cries
You covet pre-birth comfort

It persists
Traps you - frees you all at once.

You do the only thing you can
Go the place you must…
Into belly of the whale full of images;

Until it spits you out
Shaken—free.
One step nearer warm gentle memories
One inch closer sanity - for now.

It will not be denied, will return, then…
Go where you must—
To be whole - live again.

Surprise…

# No Visiting Rights

You have no visiting rights in my life

Flesh of my flesh
Blood of my blood.
Forfeited in evolution
From daddy—dad—father—stranger
Living a life unknown to me;
On a planet I cannot imagine, find.
Standing together, image memorialized
Perfect—father daughter
A joyous day—Oh!
The rest of the story;
Personification of the strange man
Money? Here? Now?

You have no visiting rights in my life
Lost, gone forever, cut out like a knife.

# Atonement

He languishes
Holds life in brown paper bag
Old wishes new rags.

He guzzles
Hurt courses through him—
What if, could, should have been?

He is dizzy
Unable to stand
Rocked by how, why, maybe I can?

He nurtures fool's elixir for uninitiated
Who drink to drown past
Powerless to enjoy strong cognac

Sip sweet aftertaste
Savor growing legs on crystal sides—
Opportunity, beliefs nearby...

He pines till drunk
Helpless to find self and know—
Person he is looking for?

Ha! Alive no more.

# Courageous Eyes

*For Serena*

Mirror prisms beg to belong
Pieced together shard by shard.

Fractured reflecting pool
Recounts scars formed long ago.

Faint glimmer of life slowly kindles
Promising flower to come,
Young woman who will be
When eclipse ends.

Wearing veil of silence,
Courageous eyes scream—

Help me...

# In The Zone

# Insomnia

It's 4 a.m.
Awake again.
Cacophony of words dancing - stumbling - turning
In my head.

It's 4 a.m.
Awake again?
Alphabet soup fight shouting—
"Take me...no me...it's my turn yet again!"

It's 4 a.m.?
Awake again!
Mother...
Betty...
So many gone since then.

It's 4 a.m.
Alive?
Awake?
Get up!
Live!

It's 4 a.m.
Write! Again.

# Six a.m.

We awake!
Awakening, sudden, cold
We lazily resist call to leave behind
Languid abyss of dreams
Aching, longing of sleepiness
Intertwined with coverings

# In The Zone

Whack!

High pitched ring—ping—chime
Masterful connection;
flesh, metal, rubber
shape-shifting

Small missile flies
filled with high hopes
dreams of birds, eagles
soars to heaven

Perfect flight rises towards target—
flags floating in breeze—
gently lands, rolls on earth
poised for greatness

Teasing, whispering - *come back tomorrow—*
*next week - return - you belong—*
Great shot!

Oh…that…felt…good!

A blessing to low aerobic athletes
A gift to age and youth

Whack!

# Dieter Delight

Savor food floating
in the moistness of your mouth
After ten pounds of lightness
months of tastelessness
sweating exercise

Savor aroma of sugary sauces
After one size smaller
clothes long forgotten - remembered
health reclaimed

Savor silky chocolate ice cream
Rolling on your tongue
And remember:

Ten pounds heavier
One size larger
Clothes forgotten
Health compromised

Savor the new you
Dieter delight!

# Spring

Cool, crisp breeze
Whispers of warmth
Gently caress eyelashes.
Elegant pointed blades of life
Push aside crusted earth
Debris of season passing.
Fists full of life grab warming sun
Bow yellow top hats to growing crowd.
Scattered bouquets of scent
Promise long days, warm nights
Invite inside out.

# Tree

Large body motionless
against a starlit night

Transfixed by nature
to single spot

Yet alive, breathing,
growing, being

Clothed in leaves first
green, then gold, then brown

Finally decked in regal
coat of ermine

Patiently waiting for
new life - Spring

# Sea

Glows, shines, radiant hue
Every color reflected in rainbow
Foams—thunders in until
Kisses the shore
Rolls away again
Beacons—*come get your fill*
Solemn peace, serenity it offers all.

Go to the sea now
Hold out your palms
Let it engulf you in its arms
Feel warmth to be had by all.

# Sun

The sun sets
With it go hopes,
Sorrows of day

The moon rises
With it comes
**Dawning of night**

# Mother Haiku

i

silence, you and me on grandma's quilt
nursing stomach cramps
warm sherry

ii

night fever stalks—
cool vick's vapo-rub gently smoothed
on five-year-old chest

iii

shadows fill with ghosts—
your whispers, gentle touch
soothe

iv

flower dressed stone marker
guards death ashes
of your life

v

*always proud…*
whispers in motherless ears
gentle as baby breath

vi

storyteller weaves family tales
rich as chocolate icing
licked from bowl

vii

i do not need
to hear an answer
just the sound of your voice

## viii

i write these poems for you
you make me
who I am

ix

words flow
as magically as fingers
moving across a wee gee board

# Safe and Sound

# Nine Eleven

we
are your
children...

your
newly
dead...

born
from
our
past...

victims
of
your
present...

Pray,

we
are
not
your
future...

# Safe and Sound

When we had it, we did not think about it
it was simply there,
sure as clean air, running water
We wrapped ourselves in its comfort
with as much ease as slipping into deep sleep,
warm covers gently pulled over our heads
soft pillow inviting us to let go, give in

We heard stories of how others do not have it,
saw images of the others absence
of basic comfort, surety, take-it-for-grantedness
But we—we had it,
the denied ones were so far away
faint apparitions of loss,
disappointment, infringement
easy to wipe from our eyes...

Nowadays, we no longer have it
not as clearly as before
not as assuredly anymore
Apparitions take solid form
mirror images of those with whom
we are intimately acquainted...

# Why Not...

Twenty-one year old nephew
writes a will
(orders from superiors)
identify who receives remains
of life not yet lived

I am old enough to remember—
nations torn asunder
twenty-nine years before...

# Harmony

Joining of hearts
Of hands
Of minds
Bearing the burden
Accepting the task
Fighting for beliefs
Living for a cause
Toiling together
Exercising as one
Loving
Living
Being till done.

# Voice

Yes!

Full, colorful springtime peonies
Sure as Mother's love
Crystal clear Carolina blue skies
Warm down-filled blanket
Committed—*I do*
Passionate fevered tributary rushing to open sea

Such stunning sound!
Oh precious journey lays in wait
Speak the one voice
Possessing right to be heard

# Prose

# Where I Belong

This is where my journey begins, my new life as a writer. How delightful to tap creative juices and nurture my imagination in such a freeing way.

However when I set out on this adventure of pursuing a writing life; which is quickly becoming an emerging lifestyle; I did not anticipate loneliness. A deep bottomless pit of emptiness which at times seems to only be occupied with the flesh, blood, bones of my body, images of my imagination, feelings of my heart.

The loneliness pulls at my psyche like a bad addiction. It keeps lingering, will not let go. Even though my mind says I should walk away – let me free. My instincts hold me in place as steadfastly as a bookmark keeps the pages and chapters yet to be read separate from words already savored. The loneliness persists.

I call it "self-prescribed aloneness" - it needs a name. I am at the creative juncture where the piece of paper remains blank, the computer screen has nothing to offer except an annoying blinking curser on a sterile white background, and my mind can not come up with words to shape, roll or play with and rearrange on the page.

I want to read aloud to myself, hear the sound of words in my ears, taste the words, feel their texture on my tongue. This helps me recognize where I need to make changes so I do not stub my toe against unintended rough edges in the language chain, stumble and trip. But the curser stares back at me. It is uncaring, mute.

I find myself at the stove, cleaning the impossible to reach places in the kitchen. Lifting up the knobs which control the on and off switches for the burners; scraping away clumps of grease stuck in-between each knob. This grease has probably been there for a decade, and but for my feeling lonely with nothing to write, would continue to live undisturbed in the shadows.

Next I find myself at the outside barbeque grill - my husband's sacred territory. I pull the cover off, heat the grill up, scrape debris of wonderful meals we enjoyed all summer long, dig along the sides of each grate for hidden remnants that always escape during a surface clean.

I am proud of myself for getting down to the black metal. I wonder if my husband will appreciate how clean the grill is when next he places steaks or salmon on the fire. However I know he probably will not notice. The days are getting shorter and when he uses the grill again it will be dark outside with only the deck spotlight to display the freshly cleaned grates.

As I step back and admire how neat and organized my closet now looks – clothes I will not wear during the impending season have been put away; things which no longer fit have been carefully folded and placed in a bag for Goodwill or the Salvation Army – I know I am in trouble.

When I have procrastinated all I can. When I have tried to escape aloneness with every ounce of energy in my bones. When I am prepared to stare the solitude in its eyes, it is then I recognize – it is the loneliness I must embrace. The quiet is where my writing life resides.

I took the first step on this journey not realizing that heading down this road would mean accepting personal loss. I am walking a path which none of my friends or family are walking with me. My lonesomeness comes from missing the very people who have been with me on all the other paths of my life. This road is littered with loss like the forested walking trail in the backyard which is strewn with fallen autumn leaves.

Sometimes I think family and friends look at me and see a second head on my body. Their head tilts to the side to get a better angle as they try to figure out – what is it? What has she grown on the other side of her head, the head we know and understand and can relate to? What is this other "thing"?

*All God's Children Need Traveling Feet,* is the title of one of Maya Angelou's books about leaving home to find home. My feet are traveling, driven by my soul and heart which has me marching along this path less traveled. Although it may be foreign to so many in my life, it feels so right for me.

So I must go into the solitude. And when it feels the deepest, that is when I am ready to write the best. It matters not that as I look back and down at the road there is but a single pair of footprints creasing the sand or snow, crushing the dried leaves on this particular corridor. It is my path.

I will take my traveling feet and move. I yearn to dance, skip, enjoy every stone that gets upturned, every twig I step over or upon, every sunset, every leaf that falls from a gold encrusted tree, each snowflake, rain drop, new friend, and evolving relationships with old ones. I will rejoice in all bursts of newness.

I know in my heart, the second head others sometimes see on my shoulder is actually an angel – a very proud mother keeping her daughter company. She is guiding these nomadic feet.

# Fifty Takes Ten

She is not unexpected yet she appears much sooner than the others anticipate. Fifty is just suddenly here, rounder than Thirty or Forty, with silver dusting in her hair, interesting lines on her face. Forty dreads seeing these lines emerge, so she avoids looking too closely at her face. However Fifty wears the lines with an air of pride, as if to say "They are me."

Ten has been waiting a long time for the others to arrive. She quietly sits on a small rocking chair behind Twenty, Thirty and Forty, patiently waiting, humming and playing with the frayed stuffed Teddy bear she always clings to at times like this – uncomfortable moments watching grownups being, well – grownup.

She likes the looks of Fifty; although she can do without the others. Twenty is O.K. but she seems a little lost. Ten envisions Twenty skipping down an uncertain path searching for people, places or things she can hold onto and call her own. Twenty wears her hair in the Diana Ross smooth glamorous look one month and then becomes an Angela Davis look-alike the next with a huge afro. And finally she returns to the silky Ross style as she steps onto the first rung of the ladder to corporate success. At one time, Twenty could sing all the lines to "The Revolution Will Not be Televised".

Thirty, well Ten does not have much time for her; probably because Thirty acts as though Ten does not exist, as though Thirty just appeared on the middle rung of the corporate ladder all by herself – immaculate conception of an executive. Thirty has laser-like focus – on success, money, being accepted, on just about anything and anyone who has nothing to do with who she is as a person. Thirty is lost, just like Twenty, although in a different way. But – she has a great career! Not much of a social life, which makes a mess for Forty to deal with.

Forty does deal with it, she has to. Ten feels a little sorry for Forty. She is beginning to wake up, get some sight back only to see the messes Thirty left for her. But Forty is cool. She recovers from Thirty's questionable relationships, softens her laser-like focus – although this is primarily due to Eyeglasses who have entered her life. Forty is not happy about needing Eyeglasses. However she has learned to use Eyeglasses strategically. When she notices the uninvited hairs on the space between the bottom of her nose and her upper lip, she begins to deny Eyeglasses access to the bathroom with her.

Eyeglasses are not invited into the garden either. As Forty is weeding and turning the soil, trimming dead stems off roses or black-eyed susies – lonely Eyeglasses rest atop the kitchen counter. They are content though, knowing as soon as Forty gets ready to read a label, magazine or book, Eyeglasses will once again snuggle tightly on the bridge of Forty's nose. But for Forty, leaving Eyeglasses inside while gardening has a way of making the backyard look almost bug and worm free.

Forty is expecting Fifty; more than Twenty or Thirty ever do. But for Forty, the expectation brings mixed emotions. On one hand it is good to know there will be Fifty. Others did not get to meet Fifty, which makes Forty sad to think about them and their families.

Yet for Forty, seeing Fifty marks the ultimate threshold to significant change. Knees, Joints, Back all speak with new, louder voices. Stomach is always shape-shifting. And Memory, oh how frustrated Forty gets, standing in the middle of a room, looking at nothing, trying to get Memory to work, do what it is supposed to do! Frustrating…

*Yes*, Ten chuckles to herself as she peaks into Forty's mind, *I do like Forty*.

"Hello, Ten." Fifty startles Ten with this greeting.

"Hi. You're Fifty, and you're talking to me."

"Yes, I'm Fifty. Why are you surprised I'm chatting with you?"

"Because none of the others speak to me. They pretend I don't exist, or they want to forget me, like they're ashamed or something."

"Well, I want to know you." Fifty reassures Ten.

"Great! Can I hold your hand?"

"Yes. Will you walk with me?"

"Sure. Where're we going?"

"I think it may be a good idea to start walking to Sixty, find out where she lives. And maybe help her plan life as she travels to Seventy."

"Wow that sounds like fun. What about the others, do they have to come along?"

"No, I don't think so. They've done their work. It's time for them to rest."

"But what about me, I'm Ten, shouldn't I be resting too?"

"Oh, no. The others didn't let you do your job. However I need to put you to work. Now is your time for me. I want to know you, bring you into my life."

"I'm glad they're not coming, I didn't really like them. Well, maybe Forty, a little. But I do like you."

"Well, they are me; who I have been. I can't deny them because they are inside. It's like a stew simmering in a big pot. The ingredients get put in one at a time, in a certain order. You stir the mixture and let it simmer for a long time. The longer it simmers, the better it tastes, and there isn't any one ingredient that stands out, the stew is now a fusion of everything. That's how it is with me and them and you. I am Fifty stew, tasting and smelling so – good and delicious." Fifty lets out a deep laugh.

"You're funny. Will you take care of me?"

"Oh, yes. I plan to take very good care of you, you deserve it...no – I deserve it."

"I promise too...to take care of you, Fifty. We can play hop scotch, marbles, tag, and jump rope, tell jokes, and just laugh a lot, all that fun stuff."

"Laugh... yes, I like that. Tell me, Ten, do you have a Mister Potato Head? I just received a gift of the new and improved fifty-year old version. He's plastic. You don't need to use a real potato to make all the faces for him or Mrs. Potato Head. It's fun."

"Fun...Plastic? Yuck... Why not use a real potato? It feels so good in my hand. All those bumps and little white things that stick out all over. When I put his nose or ears on, juice from the potato oozes on my fingers, then potato smell is everywhere. I can smell it now, just talking about it. Why plastic? Ugh!"

"Because it's new and improved, I guess."

"Fifty, is *new* better?"

"Ouch…Good question, Ten."

"Fifty, you *are* funny. C'mon, I think you better stay real close to me. I'll teach you how to feel and smell the good things in life – like *real* potatoes. Remember, you're responsible for getting us to Sixty. That road can't be paved with plastic. Ugh…"

# ABOUT THE AUTHOR

JENNIFER SMITH TURNER is a New England born writer. She began writing poetry thirty years ago while a student at Union College in Schenectady, New York. *Perennial Secrets* is her first book-length collection of poetry. Her range of verse is eclectic in the hundreds of poems she has written. Recently her work has been selected for inclusion in *Vineyard Poets*, an anthology of poems by Vineyard writers. Several of her poems and essays have been published in *The Martha's Vineyard Gazette*. Jennifer Smith Turner is a graduate of Union College, where she earned a Bachelors degree. She received her Masters degree in Communications from Fairfield University, Fairfield, CT. Subsequent to her studies she spent twenty-eight years in corporate America holding numerous senior executive positions. She is a member of the Poetry Society of America and serves on boards of many academic and non-profit organizations across the country. Jennifer resides in Connecticut and Martha's Vineyard with her husband.

www.jennifersmithturner.com

# ORDER FORM
## (Cut out and mail or fax)

PERENNIAL SECRETS, POETRY & PROSE
By
Jennifer Smith Turner

---

HARDCOVER BOOKS – #_____x $25.95 = _____

SOFTCOVER BOOKS – #_____x $15.95 = _____
(Add $4 shipping/handling per book)

(Ct. Residents add 6% sales tax)              _____

TOTAL        $ _____

## MAILING INFORMATION:

Name: _____

Address: _____

City: _____

State: _____Zip_____

Email: _____

Make check or money order payable to:  **Smith & Associates**

**Send To:**

PO Box 271753, West Hartford, CT 06127
860-284-9685 (phone/fax)

Contact jstinfo@jennifersmithturner.com for information on discounts, quantity purchases and fundraising events.

www.jennifersmithturner.com

## PERMISSION TO QUOTE

If you have comments about *Perennial Secrets, Poetry & Prose*, which I may post on my website to share with others, please write them below or email to jstinfo@jennifersmithturner.com.

_____

_____

_____

_____

_____

_____

By signing this, you agree to being quoted on the website – www.jennifersmithturner.com – or in any other promotional material related to *Perennial Secrets, Poetry & Prose*.

Name:

Contact Information:

Signature:

_____

Mail to – Smith & Associates; PO Box 271753; West Hartford, CT 06127

Fax – 860-284-9685

**THANK YOU!**                    *Jennifer Smith Turner*

Printed in the United States
1265600003B/29-115